LET'S TALK ABOUT

Drugs

Sarah Levete

Stargazer Books

© Aladdin Books Ltd 2007

Designed and produced by
Aladdin Books Ltd

First published in the
United States in 2007 by
Stargazer Books
c/o The Creative Company
123 South Broad Street
P.O. Box 227
Mankato, Minnesota 56002

Design:
Flick, Book Design and Graphics

Picture Research: Brian Hunter Smart

Editor: Jim Pipe

The consultant, David Uffindall, is a
Drugs Education Consultant with a
Local Education Authority.

*Library of Congress Cataloging- in-
Publication Data*

   Levete, Sarah.
   Drugs / by Sarah Levete.
      p. cm. -- (Let's talk about)
   Includes index.
   ISBN 978-1-59604-090-8
      1. Drug abuse--United States--Prevention--
Juvenile literature. 2. Drugs--Juvenile literature.
I. Title. II. Let's talk about (Stargazer Books (Firm))

HV5824.C45L47 2006
613.8--dc22
                                          2006009023

Contents

"Why should I know about drugs?"

You may have heard confusing things about drugs. Some people say that drugs kill. Others say that drugs from a doctor save lives. Both are right. Drugs such as medicines can help people get better. But other drugs, including illegal drugs, can be harmful and can even kill people. So too can medicines and alcohol, if not used properly.

Drugs are all around you. They include the caffeine in coffee, the alcohol in beer, and the chemicals in medicines.

This book helps to answer your questions about drugs. It tells you about the effect drugs can have on a person's body and life.

Understanding the issues will help you make clear and safe choices as you grow up.

Did you know...

Drugs mean different things to different people. To a drug dealer, illegal drugs are a way to make money. To a doctor, drugs can save the lives of patients. A drug inhaler to help control asthma (left) is helpful as long as the patient follows the doctor's instructions. But all drugs, including medicines, can be dangerous if taken the wrong way.

"What is a drug?"

Like food, drugs are taken into the body. They can change the way your body works and how you behave.

Drugs come in many forms, such as pills, creams, or liquids, some of which are injected with a needle. Some are swallowed, like the medicine you may take to fight an illness. Others are breathed in, such as inhalants.

Everyday drugs include alcohol and the nicotine in tobacco. The caffeine in some soft drinks can make you more alert or make sleeping difficult.

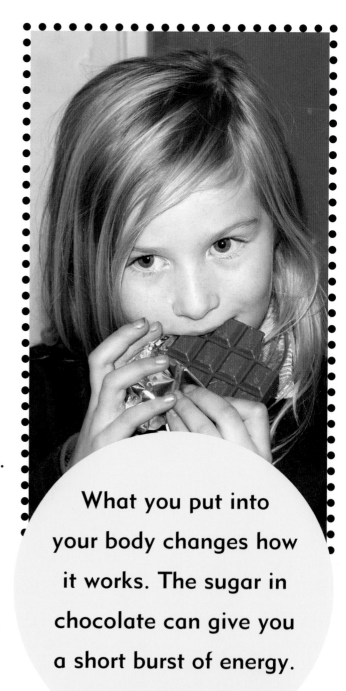

What you put into your body changes how it works. The sugar in chocolate can give you a short burst of energy.

Powerful drugs that help control illness or help deal with depression are only available on prescription from the doctor. Other drugs can be bought from a drugstore, such as painkillers to help ease a headache.

Illegal drugs, such as speed or ecstasy, are obtained from a dealer. These drugs change the way a person feels but have no medical benefit.

Think about it

Some illegal drugs, such as cannabis, are made from plants. Others, such as ecstasy, are made from chemicals. Medical drugs are made from plants or chemicals to a safe and tested formula, unlike illegal drugs.

A person using illegal drugs is never sure what the drug is made of or how strong it is. What looks like cannabis (below) could actually be dried animal dung!

"What about drugs from a doctor?"

If you are unwell, the doctor may prescribe a drug to help you get better. Sometimes, people need to take drugs from the doctor for a long time in order to stay alive. However, even drugs from a doctor can be harmful.

Drugs from the doctor can help you recover from an illness.

If a person takes too much medicine, he or she may become seriously ill. If the patient doesn't finish the course of medicine, the illness is unlikely to clear up.

Because medical drugs are made to a carefully controlled formula, a person can be told how much to take and for how long.

Did you know...

Doctors are trained to understand the effect a drug can have on a person. Getting the right drug in the correct dose (the amount of medicine) for a person is a skilled job.

• A child should only take medicine when a responsible grown-up is present.

• Only ever take the dose recommended by the doctor or on the packet or bottle.

• Never take someone else's medicine. What is ok for one person could be harmful for another.

• Follow any instructions that come with a medicine. All drugs, including medicines, can have side-effects.

"How are medicines used the wrong way?"

When we feel sad, a surprise or a treat can help to cheer us up. But when some people feel unhappy, they need to take medical drugs to change how they feel. These drugs are only given by doctors to patients with a medical need. But people can get ahold of them illegally. They abuse the drugs, which means using them the wrong way.

People can abuse even less powerful drugs, such as painkillers from a drugstore.

Some athletes abuse drugs such as steroids to make themselves stronger, even though there is no medical need. Steroids can do a lot of damage to the user's body.

If an athlete's drug abuse is found out, he or she may be banned from sporting events for many years.

Did you know...

You may have heard of "glue-sniffing." Glues and lighter fuel are types of solvents. They are not meant to be used as drugs, but some people breathe or sniff them to feel "high." But trying to get this short rush of feeling can also lead to cold sores, being sick, or even death.

"What are illegal drugs?"

You may have heard people talking about illegal drugs. Illegal means "against the law," and people are not allowed to own or sell these drugs. Because illegal drugs are not tested like medicines, no one can ever be sure what is in them. This means that people who use an illegal drug can never be sure how the drug will affect them.

Illegal drugs are also known as street drugs because many dealers sell them on the streets.

In addition to official names, street drugs have nicknames, such as snow, E, or whizz. They make different changes to the body. Some make the user feel relaxed.

Other drugs make the person feel full of energy. All illegal drugs can damage a user's body, and some will do it quicker than others. Class A drugs are the most powerful.

Did you know...

COCAINE

A white powder that is snorted (sniffed in) or injected. This drug can be very addictive and can cause chest and heart problems. Crack cocaine is smoked. It can make users violent and is highly addictive.

HEROIN

A white powder that is injected or snorted. This drug is very addictive. Taking too much (overdosing) can lead to death. Sharing needles can also lead to dangerous infections such as HIV/AIDS.

LSD

Tiny tablets or squares of paper that are swallowed. LSD changes the way users experience the world, called "tripping." Bad trips can be very frightening or lead to mental health problems.

ECSTASY

Tablets that are swallowed. Using ecstasy can cause kidney, liver, and heart problems, tiredness, and depression. Ecstasy has been linked with brain damage. It also dehydrates the user, which means it removes fluids from the body. Drinking too much water to try to replace this lost fluid can be as risky as not drinking enough.

AMPHETAMINES

A gray or white powder. These drugs can cause anxiety or panic and may make some users feel tired and depressed.

CANNABIS

This drug can come in brown lumps known as resin, or leaves (grass). It is usually smoked, often with tobacco. Because of this, users can become addicted to cigarettes. Smoking cannabis over many years can cause memory loss or a lack of energy.

"What do drugs do?"

People may misuse a particular drug for the effect they hope it will have on their mind or body. But the effect depends on the drug, its strength, who uses it, and the place in which it is used.

For instance, a young man injecting heroin by himself could die if he injects too much and there is no one to get help. One girl taking LSD could feel alright, but her friend may have a terrifying experience.

Drugs may make a person feel happy. But they can also cause illness, accidents, and in some cases, death.

Using some drugs can create a change of mood for some people, creating a "high" or feeling of well-being. But the same drug can have the opposite effect on others.

The long-term effects can be more serious. They range from pale, pimply skin to brain damage or heart attacks.

Think about it

Regularly using drugs can change a person's body and mind so much that he or she wants more and more of them. We say they are "addicted" to drugs. The person may be unable to function without using drugs. They may do almost anything to get ahold of them, including stealing or using violence.

"What are the risks of using drugs?"

You may have overheard someone saying how much they enjoy taking drugs. But anyone who misuses drugs risks damaging their mind and body, especially if they take them often. If they use dirty needles to inject drugs they can also risk getting infections such as hepatitis or HIV. Smoking tobacco or illegal drugs can lead to lung cancer, even years after a person has stopped smoking.

If you see a used needle don't touch it. It could be infected. Tell an adult where you found it.

Street drugs can muddle and cloud a person's judgment. It is more likely for someone on drugs to have an accident, especially if they are near such places as railroads, rivers, or roads, or if they are driving.

Mixing different drugs or drugs and alcohol is very dangerous because it is hard to know the combined effect of the drug "cocktail." Taking too much of a drug can lead to physical collapse or even death.

Think about it

If someone uses illegal drugs, they also risk getting into trouble. Drug dealers often use violence to deal with users who cannot pay them for the drugs they have used.

Being caught with illegal drugs, sharing them, or selling them can lead to a fine, a criminal record, and even time in prison.

"Why do people take drugs?"

You may wonder why people take drugs with all the risks. But ask a parent why they or their friends drink alcohol or smoke. They may say they like the taste or the way it makes them feel.

People often try street drugs to get a "high," or just to see what it feels like. Some may start using drugs to rebel against their parents.

Drugs may seem to offer an escape from problems. But taking drugs only creates more problems.

Drugs change the way a person feels, so a person facing problems at school or at home may turn to drugs as a way to escape the difficult feelings. But drugs don't make problems disappear, and they can often cause even more difficult ones.

Some people take drugs such as ecstasy to make a night out seem more fun. But the after-effects can lead to feeling panicked or depressed, or even mental illness.

Did you know...

At some time, you will probably meet people who use drugs. You may feel under pressure to try drugs to show that you are as cool as your friends. Your friends may make you feel silly if you don't try. But think about the possible consequences. It's your life that is at stake. Making a wise, responsible, and healthy choice will leave you in control. If your friends won't accept that, are they worth it?

"Do all drug users have a drugs problem?"

You have probably heard people say that all drugs are bad. But if you see people enjoying a drink or smoking cannabis, you may wonder what is so bad about them.

Drugs cause problems when people take risks. The more you understand about them, the safer you will be.

Everyone who uses drugs runs a risk of developing a health problem or an addiction.

For instance, some people think that sniffing glue a few times won't be a problem. But they may not realize that the first time some people sniff glue it can make them black out and may even kill them.

Regularly using drugs also creates a need. To start with, a person may think he or she is in control. But soon they find that they want the drug more and more.

Street drugs are particularly risky because no one knows their strength. It is easy to take too much —and they can kill.

My Story

"My big sister started trying drugs to fit in with her friends. She started off taking a pill now and then. Soon she was taking them every day—she had become addicted. It took her a long time to come off them, and it's been really hard on all of us." Sam

"How can I say 'no' to drugs?"

No one can make you take drugs, though some people may try to persuade you. But you can say no to them. It's not always an easy thing to do, but it is a good choice.

If you are offered drugs, think about yourself rather than what others may think. To help you stand up for yourself and your life, the following tips may help:

It's your life, and it's your decision. Don't let others decide for you.

① Avoid situations where others put pressure on you.

② If someone offers you drugs, be aware of how dangerous they can be. It is up to you to keep your mind and body safe.

③ Look the other person in the eye, be confident and say "No" firmly.

④ If someone is putting you under pressure, why not practice these replies. Say clearly, "I prefer to stay in control," or, "I don't want to take a chance on a drug, especially if no one knows what it is really in it."

⑤ Remember, you can always ask advice from a grown-up that you trust.

Think about it

Involve yourself with friends who share your interests and make you feel good about yourself for who you are. Join a club or get involved in an activity that you enjoy. There are many ways to have fun with friends without taking drugs.

"How do drug users affect others?"

It is not just drug users who are affected by drugs. It is all of the people around them at home, at school, or at work.

People who regularly use drugs may feel the need for the drug so much that they cannot think about anything else. They may not care that they are ruining others' lives as well as their own.

The people closest to a person with a drug problem suffer the most.

Drugs cost a lot of money. If someone needs to spend a lot of money on drugs it means they may get into financial difficulty. They may even lose their home. Children playing in an area where people use drugs could hurt themselves on needles with which drug users have injected drugs. The children could even catch a serious infection from the needles.

My story

"I've always been really close to my big sister Lisa. But then she started taking drugs. She says they make her feel good, but I think they just make her lose control. I've even seen her attacking her friends. She's also stealing from Mom to pay for them. I'm really worried about Lisa, but she won't listen. It is really upsetting me." Ronan

"Why can it be hard to give up drugs?"

Young people who try drugs may think it is easy to stop taking them. If they are lucky, they may try a drug once or twice and find they can stop without much difficulty.

But many drugs are addictive. Regular drug users can find it very hard to give up. It can be very painful as their body has to get used to being without the drug.

Coming off drugs is hard work. But in time, people can start to enjoy their lives again.

Even when people have come off drugs, they have to learn to deal with problems without depending on drugs to escape.

Some drug users have to avoid meeting people and going to places where they may be tempted to misuse drugs again. They may even have to leave their home and friends and start a new life somewhere else.

Did you know...

People coming off drugs need a lot of support. Their families may need support, too. There are many sources of help. Self-help groups run by former drug users offer addicts encouragement and understanding. Some people may need medicine from the doctor to help handle the painful symptoms of giving up drugs.

"What if someone I know takes drugs?"

If someone close to you is using drugs, and it is affecting you, talk to a grown-up you trust, such as a teacher or parent.

Letting someone know about another person with a drug problem is not tattling, and it could save someone's life.

Telling someone about a person's drug abuse could save a life.

If you are being put under pressure from people around you to take drugs, tell a grown-up you trust. They will be understanding and will help you stand up for yourself. If you are tempted by drugs, think about what you are doing and the risks you might be taking. Talk to someone you trust to find the support you may need.

Think about it

A lot of people are tempted to take drugs. Some do so without serious problems. For others, it can ruin their lives and those of their families. Talking to someone about drug abuse can help the person with the problem and those around them.

"What can I do?"

• Unless you are ill, you do not need drugs. If you eat and sleep well, your body can usually look after itself.

• It's how people use drugs that causes problems. Medical drugs can fight illness, but they can also cause addiction and even death if they are abused.

• Choose friends and activities that don't involve drugs.

• If people offer you drugs, think about the risks, not just the short-term feelings the drugs may give. Be clear about your choice to say "No," and feel good about it.

Enjoy life without the problems that drugs can cause.

Books on drugs

If you want to read more about drugs, try:

The *Your Body and Health* series by
Jen Green (Stargazer)
Choices and Decisions: Taking Drugs by
Pete Sanders & Steve Myers (Stargazer)

On the Web

These websites are also helpful:

www.focusas.com/SubstanceAbuse.html
www.dare.com/index_3.htm
www.drugabuse.com
www.thesite.org

Contact information

If you want to talk to someone who doesn't
know you, these organizations can help:

Narcotics Anonymous
P.O. Box 9999
Van Nuys, CA 91409 USA
Tel: (818) 773-9999
www.na.org

Canadian Center for Substance Abuse
75 Alberta Street, Suite 300
Ottawa, ON K1P 5E7 Canada
Tel: (613) 235-8101
www.ccsa.ca

National Youth Anti-Drug Media Campaign
P.O. Box 6000, Rockville
MD 20849–6000 USA
Tel: (800) 666-3332
www.mediacampaign.org

**Partnership for a Drug
Free America**
405 Lexington Ave.
Suite 1601, NYC,
NY 10174 USA
www.drugfree-
america.org

Teen Drug Abuse
13223 Ventura
  Boulevard, Suite E
Studio City, CA 91604 USA
Tel: (866) 784-8411
www.teen-drug-abuse.org

Teen Challenge International
3728 W. Chestnut Expressway
Springfield, MO 65802 USA
Tel: (417) 862-6969
www.teenchallenge.com

There is lots
of useful
information
about drugs on
the internet.

Index

Photocredits

The publishers would like to acknowledge that the photographs reproduced in this book have been posed by models or have been obtained from photographic agencies.
Abbreviations: l-left, r-right, b-bottom, t-top, c-center, m-middle
All photos supplied by PBD except for:Front cover, 3tr, 3mr, 5bl — Select Pictures. 1, 5tr, 7tl, 15b — Corbis. 2 — Brand X Pictures. 3br, 18r, 19b — Image 100. 4 — Flat Earth. 7br — US Department of Justice; DEA. 9tl, 23br, 30r — Photodisc. 10bl, 12b, 26b, 27b, 28b — Roger Vlitos. 11tl — Corel. 14r, 20r, 25br — Image State.